CURSIVE WRITING
Sentences

Ages: 4-6 years

This book belongs to

MOONSTONE

Ask grandma to wake up.

Ask grandma to wake up.

Ask grandma to wake up.

Ask grandma to wake up.

Ask grandma to wake up.

Don't play in the dark.

Don't play in the dark.

Don't play in the dark.

Don't play in the dark.

Don't play in the dark.

Please get me some cheese from the fridge.

Please get me some cheese from the fridge.

Please get me some cheese from the fridge.

Please get me some cheese from the fridge.

Please get me some cheese from the fridge.

The kite will go up in the sky if it's windy.

The kite will go up in the sky if it's windy.

The kite will go up in the sky if it's windy.

The kite will go up in the sky if it's windy.

The kite will go up in the sky if it's windy.

Please take the dog out for a walk.

Please take the dog out for a walk.

Please take the dog out for a walk.

Please take the dog out for a walk.

Please take the dog out for a walk.

Mother is sitting on the sofa.

Mother is sitting on the sofa.

Mother is sitting on the sofa.

Mother is sitting on the sofa.

Mother is sitting on the sofa.

Use a pencil to mark the answers.

Use a pencil to mark the answers.

Use a pencil to mark the answers.

Use a pencil to mark the answers.

Use a pencil to mark the answers.

It's time to go to bed.

It's time to go to bed.

It's time to go to bed.

It's time to go to bed.

It's time to go to bed.

Don't go out in this weather.

Don't go out in this weather.

Don't go out in this weather.

Don't go out in this weather.

Don't go out in this weather.

Write down the things you saw at the farm.

Write down the things you saw at the farm.

Write down the things you saw at the farm.

Write down the things you saw at the farm.

Write down the things you saw at the farm.

I can see a baby crawling.

I can see a baby crawling.

I can see a baby crawling.

I can see a baby crawling.

I can see a baby crawling.

Write down your sibling's name.

Write down your sibling's name.

Write down your sibling's name.

Write down your sibling's name.

Write down your sibling's name.

There is a bag on the table.

There is a bag on the table.

There is a bag on the table.

There is a bag on the table.

There is a bag on the table.

Let's play hide-and-seek today.

Let's play hide-and-seek today.

Let's play hide-and-seek today.

Let's play hide-and-seek today.

Let's play hide-and-seek today.

You should share your toys.

You should share your toys.

You should share your toys.

You should share your toys.

You should share your toys.

I saw a shooting star last night.

I saw a shooting star last night.

I saw a shooting star last night.

I saw a shooting star last night.

I saw a shooting star last night.

Playing with friends is a good activity.

Playing with friends is a good activity.

Playing with friends is a good activity.

Playing with friends is a good activity.

Playing with friends is a good activity.

The dog will fetch the wooden stick.

The dog will fetch the wooden stick.

The dog will fetch the wooden stick.

The dog will fetch the wooden stick.

The dog will fetch the wooden stick.

Everyone has to wear a red cap tomorrow.

Everyone has to wear a red cap tomorrow.

Everyone has to wear a red cap tomorrow.

Everyone has to wear a red cap tomorrow.

Everyone has to wear a red cap tomorrow.

Lemonade will relieve the heat stroke.

Lemonade will relieve the heat stroke.

Lemonade will relieve the heat stroke.

Lemonade will relieve the heat stroke.

Lemonade will relieve the heat stroke.

We spotted a tiger in the zoo.

We spotted a tiger in the zoo.

We spotted a tiger in the zoo.

We spotted a tiger in the zoo.

We spotted a tiger in the zoo.

Baby monkey was sleeping in the afternoon.

Baby monkey was sleeping in the afternoon.

Baby monkey was sleeping in the afternoon.

Baby monkey was sleeping in the afternoon.

Baby monkey was sleeping in the afternoon.

The cat ran faster than the dog.

The cat ran faster than the dog.

The cat ran faster than the dog.

The cat ran faster than the dog.

The cat ran faster than the dog.

Complete your homework in time.

Complete your homework in time.

Complete your homework in time.

Complete your homework in time.

Complete your homework in time.

Let's get ice cream for everyone.

Let's get ice cream for everyone.

Let's get ice cream for everyone.

Let's get ice cream for everyone.

Let's get ice cream for everyone.

This box will fit in my bag.

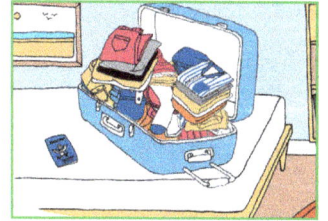

This box will fit in my bag.

This box will fit in my bag.

This box will fit in my bag.

This box will fit in my bag.

I painted this picture.

I painted this picture.

I painted this picture.

I painted this picture.

I painted this picture.

Please read this story again.

Please read this story again.

Please read this story again.

Please read this story again.

Please read this story again.

We will learn how to make a paper boat today.

We will learn how to make a paper boat today.

We will learn how to make a paper boat today.

We will learn how to make a paper boat today.

We will learn how to make a paper boat today.

This is my childhood friend.

This is my childhood friend.

This is my childhood friend.

This is my childhood friend.

This is my childhood friend.

Brushing twice a day is a good habit.

Brushing twice a day is a good habit.

Brushing twice a day is a good habit.

Brushing twice a day is a good habit.

Brushing twice a day is a good habit.